Cane and Rush Seating — a practical guide

Cane and Rush Seating
— a practical guide

David & Freda Broan

Bishopsgate Press Ltd.
37 Union Street, London, SE1 1SE

Printed by Whitstable Litho Ltd., Millstrood Road, Whitstable, Kent.

Contents

Introduction

Cane and rush seating belong to a tradition that has been handed down over many generations of chair making.

The two crafts, although found in many different forms, employ relatively simple techniques requiring little in the way of tools and equipment. They are therefore ideally suitable for someone wishing to take up a satisfying and rewarding hobby.

Many homes contain examples of the two styles of seating, often, due to their age, in a sad state of disrepair. The restoration of such pieces to a useful and attractive life is worthwhile in itself, but taking into consideration the poor quality and high price of much contemporary furniture, it also makes sound economic sense.

The aim of this book is to explain in simple terms the method of working for as wide a variety of seats as possible, the accompanying pictures providing a step by step visual check on the work done.

This should enable even a complete beginner to produce a satisfactory result at the first attempt. The knowledge that the finished work will last for several generations, given reasonable use, is an added source of pleasure.

There is also included a section dealing with the modern technique of chair seating using a machine made web of cane. While the results obtained by this method are in no way comparable with a traditionally woven seat, it is included because of its present popularity in order that such chairs can be repaired.

Dining Chair

This attractive dining chair with spiral twist middle rail was one of a set of six, all of which needed restoration and repair.

Although the seat frame was wider at the front than at the back, the number of caning holes at front and back was the same, the difference being taken up by wider spacing of the holes in the front rail.

The first step was to note the details of the original seat as this was intact. (figure 1). The following points were observed.

1. Size of cane used (see chapter 15)
2. Caning pattern used (see chapter 15)
3. Size and type of beading

In this chair No 2 cane was used for the canes running from front to back and from side to side of the seat (Settings)

No 3 cane was used for the canes running diagonally. (Crossings).

The standard 'double setting' pattern was used (see chapter 15) as illustrated in figure 2.

The seat was beaded with No 6 cane and couched with No 2.

Preparation of Frame:

The old web of cane was removed from the seat by cutting closely around the inside of the frame with a sharp knife. Care must be taken not to damage the wood of the frame while this is being done. The old seat should be kept for reference purposes and for eventual colour matching if required.

Next the old cane and any pegs were removed from the frame holes (see chapter 18) using the clearing tool and a light hammer.

1. Original condition of seat.

2. Double setting pattern.

1

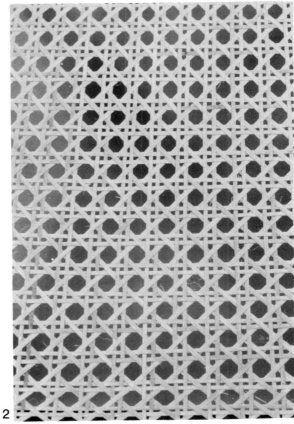

2

The tool should always be used from underneath the frame to avoid the possibility of accidental damage to the rail surface.

The frame was then wiped clean of dust with a soft rag moistened with a little turpentine. Often it will be found that the colour of the wood has deteriorated where it has been overlaid by the cane. This may be restored by substituting a little spirit stain of a suitable colour for the turpentine.

Finally the frame was buffed with a rag containing a little beeswax polish.

First Settings:

The first stage in recaning was to put in the first settings, which are the canes running from front to back of the seat in pairs.

Two pieces of No 2 cane of good length were chosen and examined for flaws. The end of the first was inserted down through the centre hole in the back rail, being held in position with a peg, leaving about 6" below the rail. (see figure 3 A).

The cane was then brought forward and taken down through the centre hole in the front rail (figure 3 B) and pegged, then brought up again through the next hole to the left (figure 3 C) and again pegged.

The shiny side of the cane must always be kept uppermost and care should be taken that it does not become twisted in the holes or under the seat.

The cane was then taken across the seat and down through the opposite hole in the back rail (figure 3 D) then up through the next hole to the left (figure 3 E) and so on.

The second cane of the first setting starts from the centre hole of the front rail (figure 4 B) and travels in the opposite direction to the first cane, i.e. (looking at figure 4) across the seat and down through hole A, up through

3. *Course of first cane of first setting.*

4. *Course of second cane of first setting.*

10

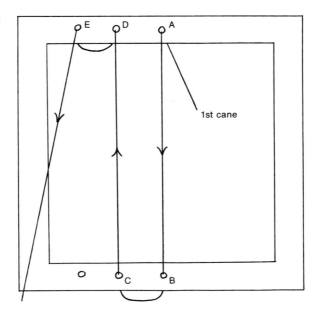

3

1st cane

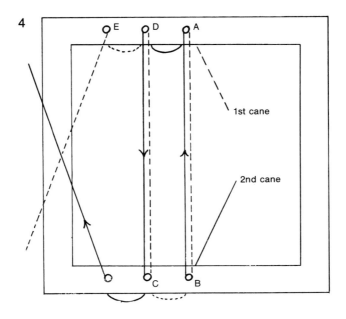

4

1st cane

2nd cane

hole D, across and down through hole C and so on.

Four pegs are needed at this stage; two which remain in the centre holes, and two which proceed with the work.

The work should be firm but not pulled tight nor should it become slack. When the end of a length of cane is reached, a new piece may be joined in.

The end of the old cane is brought up through the next hole in the rail as usual and the end of the new cane is inserted down through the hole and is knotted onto the loop of the old cane underneath (see figure 5). The knot must be tight and care must be taken that it is not pulled up into the hole when the slack is taken up. Always hold the tail of the old cane whilst tightening the new one. The correct final position for the knot is shown in figure 6.

The work was continued in this way until the left hand rail was reached. New lengths of cane were then joined in at the centre of the seat and the right hand half of the first settings were put in similarly. The first setting stage is shown in figure 7 almost complete.

At this stage check that all the canes are the right way up (shiny side uppermost) and are not twisted or crossed, but lie flat and parallel to one another across the full depth of the seat.

Second Settings:

The second settings run at right angles to the first, i.e. from side to side of the seat, and are woven into the first settings to form the basic supporting web of cane.

5. *Tying in a new length of cane*

6. *Correct final position of knot under frame*

7. *First setting stage almost complete.*

5

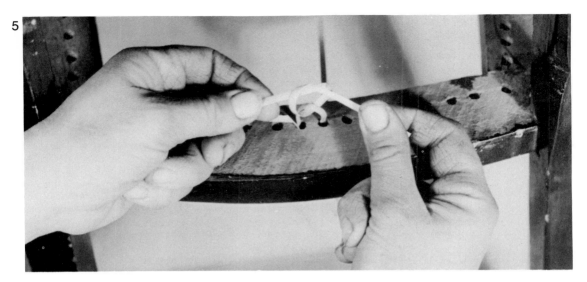

6

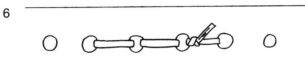

7

If there are long 'tails' of cane left over from where the first settings finish, they may often be brought back up through the first holes in the side rails and used to commence the second settings. Otherwise new pieces must be inserted.

The second settings are worked in the same way as the first but are woven alternately under and over the first setting canes all the way across the seat.

Start from the first hole in the left hand rail and weave under-over, under-over, all the way across to the first hole in the right hand rail. Then take the other cane of the pair from the first hole in the right hand rail, under-over, under-over, all the way across to the left hand rail. This will give you the basic pattern of the settings (see figure 8) and should be continued through to the back of the seat, new lengths of cane being tied in as needed.

Sometimes it is easier to work some of the second settings from the back of the chair and to meet in the middle. If this is done care must be taken to start from the right hand rail at the back or the pattern will not be the same.

As each pair of canes is inserted they must be pulled down into place so that they run straight across from side to side of the seat and should be pulled gently but firmly to take up any slack.

As the work proceeds it will 'tighten up' until with the stage complete the web of cane will be stretched tightly across the seat frame.

Figure 9 shows the chair after all the second settings had been put in in this way.

It is as well to check regularly for errors in the pattern of weaving as they spoil the overall appearance of the finished work and tend to weaken the seat.

8. *Pattern of weaving formed by the settings.*

9. *Second setting stage complete.*

14

8

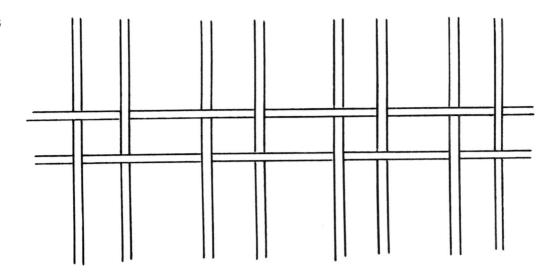

9

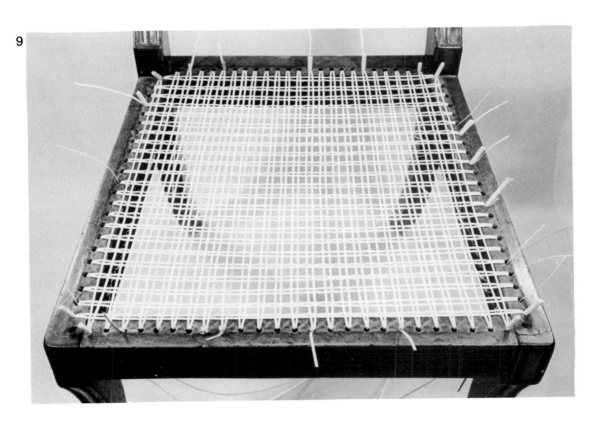

First Crossings:

Having completed the settings the next stage was to put in the first crossings, that is the single canes running diagonally across the seat frame.

No 3 cane was used and work was commenced from the front left hand corner hole in the frame. The cane was woven diagonally over the first pair of first settings and under the first pair of second settings and then so on towards the back right hand corner of the seat.

It should be noted that the cane should slip quite easily and snugly between the first and second settings where they cross. If it does not, then it means that the original pattern of weaving was reversed and therefore the crossing pattern must be reversed to match. This means that you must weave under the first settings and over the second settings. If you try both ways it will be quite obvious which is correct.

The crossings may be put in in one continuous length where convenient or may be put in singly. New canes need not be tied in. Whichever method is used, all ends should be left long enough (1½–2'') to be pulled tight when pegging or beading. Normally the corner holes each take two canes which gives a neat finish to the seat.

The completed first crossing stage is shown in figure 10.

10. First crossing stage complete.

16

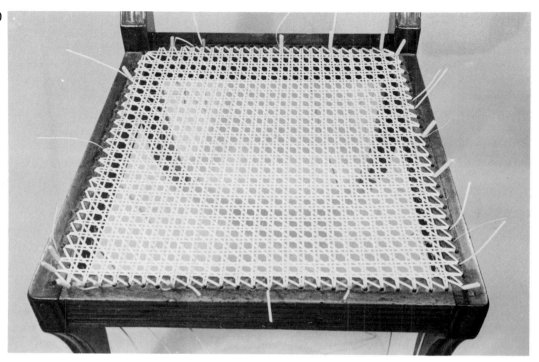

Second Crossings:

The second crossing was the final stage in weaving the seat and was carried out in a similar manner to the first crossing.

Start from the front right hand corner hole but weave under the first pair of first settings and over the first pair of second settings and so on.

Figure 11 shows the second crossing stage complete.

11. Second crossing stage complete.

Pegging and Beading:

No 6 cane was used for the beading and four lengths were cut, one for each side of the frame, allowing enough extra cane at each end to go down through the corner holes.

No 2 cane was used for the couching and several three foot lengths were prepared.

Next the holes that would not be used for couching were pegged with centre cane, the correct thickness being selected for the size of the holes (see chapter 15).

The best way to decide which holes to peg is as follows.

Firstly the corner holes are always left open to take the ends of the beading cane itself. Next, starting from the front left hand corner, work along the front rail, leaving the first after the corner hole open and then pegging every other hole. Then work back along each of the side rails in the same way and finally along the back rail from right to left.

Figure 12 shows pegging in progress.

12. Pegging the seat prior to beading.

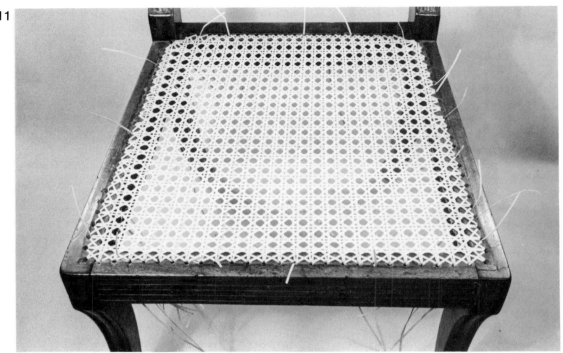

11

12

The front length of beading cane was now loosely inserted being held in place at the left hand end with a peg.

The end of a length of couching cane was inserted down through the first hole in the front rail and was tied onto the work under the frame. The other end of the cane was then taken over the beading cane and back down through the same hole, then along under the rail and up through the third hole and so on (see figure 13).

Always be sure that the cane is shiny side up and is kept tight, watching particularly the loops underneath. Each length of couching cane should be tied securely into the work at start and finish and care should be taken not to twist the cane in the holes or under the seat.

When the work was completed all loose ends were trimmed off neatly under the frame.

The completed chair is shown in figure 14.

13. Method of couching.

14. The finished chair.

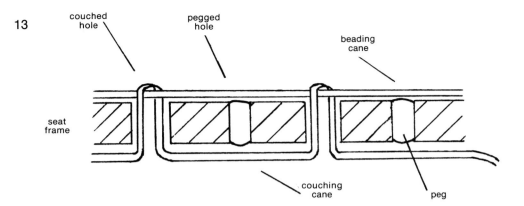

13

couched hole

pegged hole

beading cane

seat frame

couching cane

peg

14

Bedroom Chair

This little bedroom chair was one of a pair that had been caned originally in single setting pattern. As the seat of its partner was still sound, single setting pattern was again used to match.

No. 3 cane was used for the settings and No. 4 for the crossings. No. 6 cane for beading and No. 2 for couching.

The seat was not square, there being less holes in the back rail than in the front.

Preparation of Frame:

Although the seat had already been cut from the frame, the holes were still clogged with pegs and the remains of the old cane (figure 15). When these had been cleared the frame was cleaned using a little turpentine and a little spirit stain. This improved the rather 'tired' appearance of the wood and left the surface ready for later polishing.

First Settings:

In the single setting pattern (see figure 16) the settings are woven with single canes, instead of pairs of canes, between the holes.

A length of No. 3 cane was selected and as with the dining chair the work was commenced from the centre of the back rail. The same pattern of working was followed until all the holes on the back rail had been filled. This left one short setting at each side of the frame to be inserted parallel with the main settings in the seat.

Often it is possible to continue with the same piece of cane for these short settings as has been used for the rest of the seat. Otherwise they may be put in as seperate lengths and tied into the web of the seat later.

Figures 17 & 18 show the top and bottom of the seat with first setting stage complete.

15. *Original state of chair frame.*

16. *Single setting pattern.*

17. *First Setting stage (Top view)*

18. *First Setting stage (Bottom view)*

22

15

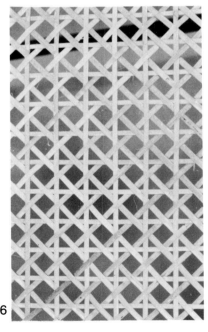

16

17

18

Second Settings:

In the single setting pattern, the second settings are not woven into the first, but are just laid on top of them to form a grid.

The work was started from the first hole in the left hand rail and was continued from side to side of the frame towards the back of the seat. The completed second setting stage is shown in figure 19.

19. Second setting stage complete

Crossings and Beading:

The first crossing was begun from the front left hand corner hole of the frame. The cane was then woven under the first settings and over the second settings across the frame to the opposite corner. It will be found that this stabilizes the web of cane and that as the work continues the seat will 'tighten up' in the normal manner.

20. Completed Chair.

With the single setting pattern the crossings should be worked in a continuous length to give extra strength to the seat. Similarly all loose ends should be tied into the work under the frame.

The second crossings were inserted as for the dining chair but were woven over the first settings and under the second settings.

Finally the seat was pegged and beaded and after trimming was stained down to match its partner.

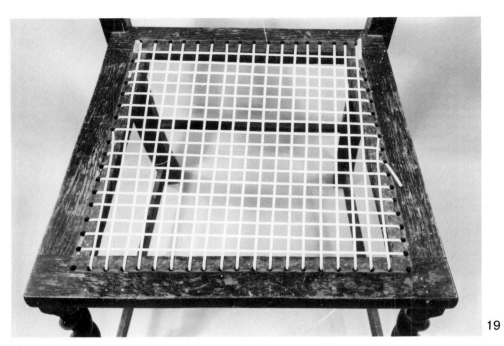

19

20

Two Bentwood Chairs with Round Seats.

Two traditional bentwood chairs, one full size, one a child's chair, both seated in double setting pattern using No. 2 cane for the settings and No. 3 for the crossings.

The beading used on a round seat is often narrower than on a square seat but in this case was standard No. 6 cane. No. 2 was used for the couching.

Settings:

Although the basic method of working the settings is the same for all seats, adjustments must be made to take account of differences in the shape of the frame.

The first step with a round seat was to find the centre holes at the back and front by counting round each way from where the back supports of the chair were attached to the seat frame.

The first settings were then commenced in the usual way between the centre holes, working across the frame to the left and then to the right. Near the outside edges of the frame it was necessary to miss out a hole in order to keep the settings an even distance apart.

Figure 22 shows the first setting stage complete.

With a round seat the second settings should be started in the centre of the seat rather than at front or back and then worked out to each edge, as with the first settings.

21. *Original condition of chairs.*

22. *First setting stage complete.*

21

22

In this respect care must be taken to keep the pattern correct. When working from the centre towards the back of the seat, start with the left hand cane of each pair weaving under-over, under-over, etc. Working from the centre towards the front of the seat start with the right hand cane of each pair and work similarly.

Again, towards the edges of the seat, a hole had to be missed out in order to keep the settings evenly spaced apart.

Figure 23 shows the second setting stage complete.

On a round seat of this kind, there is often a groove cut in the bottom of the chair frame to take the cane. Care must be taken to ensure that all knots and loops of cane under the seat fit snugly into the groove.

Crossings:

The first crossings were woven in the normal manner, starting from approximately the front left hand corner of the seat, and weaving diagonally over the first settings and under the second settings.

The second crossings were woven in a similar manner but, of course, under the first settings and over the second.

On a round seat it is often not obvious which hole a particular crossing cane should start from or finish in. There is no hard and fast rule but the aim should be for a neat finish and a natural appearance.

A consideration of figures 24 and 25 which show the first and second crossing stage respectively give an idea of what to aim for.

The crossings should be worked continuously as far as possible though this may be difficult in parts of the seat, where adjacent canes need to share the same hole.

23. Second setting stage complete

24. First crossing stage.

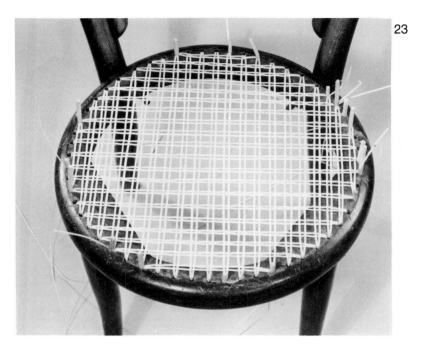

23

24

Beading:

As the beading on a round seat is continuously curved, every hole must be couched in order to keep the beading cane securely in place. Therefore none of the holes will be pegged.

A length of No. 6 cane was cut a little longer than the distance around the seat and one end was inserted down through the centre hole at the back.

Each hole was then couched in turn using No. 2 cane and working all the way around the seat until complete.

Finally the other end of the beading cane was trimmed and pushed down through the centre hole at the back of the seat which was then pegged to hold all secure.

The completed work is shown in figure 26.

25. *Second crossing stage.*

26. *The completed chairs.*

25

26

Balloon Back Chair with Shaped Seat

Although many cane seats tend to be basically square or round in outline, a number of interesting shaped examples may be met with from time to time.

In the example shown in figure 27 three extra pairs of short first setting canes were needed on each side of the seat, running from the front rail back to suitable holes in the side rails (see figure 28), parallel to the rest of the seat.

27. Original condition.

28. First settings.

27

28

Also at the second setting stage (figure 29) care had to be taken to ensure even spacing of the canes toward the front of the seat where the holes used came in the curve of the seat frame.

The crossings followed the normal pattern; the holes used for each cane being determined by the appearance and natural flow of the work.

The beading for a chair of this type is applied in two lengths. One along the back rail, and one continuous length for the rest of the seat. On the straight sections of rails alternate holes may be pegged, but on the sharply curved sections over the front legs every hole should be couched.

The finished chair is shown in figure 30. The cane sizes used were: No. 2 for settings and couching, No. 3 for crossings and No. 6 for beading.

29. Second settings.

30. Finished Seat.

29

30

Chair Backs in Cane

Chairs which have cane panels in the backs may be considered conveniently in three categories:

Firstly, chairs in which the cane panel is flat and which may therefore be worked in exactly the same manner as a seat of similar shape.

The example shown in figure 31 falls into this category and is worked exactly as for a shaped seat, making the necessary adjustments to the first and second settings to fill in neatly the shaped edges of the panel.

Secondly, chairs where the cane panel is curved in one or even two directions. For a simple curved panel, such as in figure 32, the normal method applies, but the first settings are always worked between the holes in the curved rails, in this case the first setting would run from top to bottom of the panel. This establishes the line of the curve and the second settings may then be woven in the normal manner.

The method used for a panel that is curved in two directions is shown in chapter 6.

Thirdly, chairs with more elaborate ornamental panels where special techniques are required, or where the caning holes do not go right the way through the frame of the chair. These types are also dealt with in later chapters.

31. Back with flat cane panel.

32. Back with curved panel.

31

32

Arm Chair with Curved Back

The cane panel in the back of this arm chair was unusual in that it curved two ways. This meant that the first settings, which were to run from top to bottom of the frame, had to be supported in position until after the second settings had been added. This ensured the correct curves in the finished panel.

Double setting pattern was used with No. 2 cane for the settings and No. 3 for the crossings. There was no beading and each hole was pegged.

Preparation:

When the frame had been cleared of the old cane and cleaned, the line of the two curves involved was considered and temporary supporting canes were pegged into the frame at intervals as shown in figure 34.

The relative tension of these canes was adjusted until the desired curves were obtained. Care must be taken to ensure that the pegs holding the supporting canes are really tight or they will pull out as the work proceeds.

For the size of panel that we were working on (approximately 16″ square) five horizontal and three vertical canes were used. More horizontal supports because these had to support the full weight of the first settings while the vertical supports were only to establish the line of the curve.

33. Original condition of back.

34. Back with supporting canes in place.

33

34

Settings:

The first settings were begun from the holes immediately to the left of the centre supporting cane. When the work reached the left hand supporting cane this was removed and the first settings continued until the left hand rail was reached.

Care must be taken not to distort the line of the curve as the settings are put in. Thus they must not be tightened although undue slackness is also to be avoided.

The centre vertical supporting cane was then removed, new canes joined in, and the first settings continued to the right hand rail in a similar manner. The completed first setting stage is shown in figure 35.

The second settings were then woven in the usual manner each being gently tensioned to maintain the contours of the curves in the shape desired. As the work progressed so the horizontal supporting canes were removed in turn. The second setting stage is shown in figure 36.

Crossings and Completion:

The crossing stages were now very straight forward as the frame was basically square in shape. When complete, each hole was pegged with centre cane and the work was trimmed and lightly stained. The completed chair is shown in figure 37.

35. *First Settings in place.*

36. *Second Settings in place.*

37. *Completed back.*

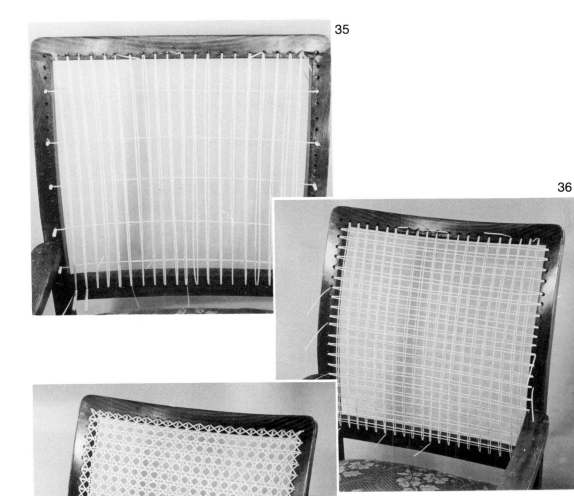

35

36

37

Cane Panel with Sunray Pattern

The sunray pattern is found from time to time in chair backs. The example shown in figure 38 was one of a pair of bedroom chairs in need of repair. No. 2 cane was used for the settings and No. 3 for the crossings.

The frame of the back was basically rectangular in shape with the characteristic semi-circular 'sun' at the centre of the bottom rail. If this sun-hub has to be cleared of old cane and pegs, great care must be taken as the holes are always very fine and very closely spaced.

The best tool for this job is a fine awl which has had the point removed from the blade. Alternatively a long fine nail with the point filed down will sometimes suffice.

First Settings:

In the sunray pattern the first settings all radiate from the sun-hub to be distributed evenly around the three sides of the frame opposite.

Because of the close proximity of the holes in the hub itself, all new lengths of cane must be joined in on the main frame of the panel and not on the hub.

Double settings are used but in this pattern the first settings are put in singly and should be kept quite tight if a satisfactory tension is to be obtained in the finished panel.

A length of No. 2 cane was inserted into the centre hole in the top rail and was brought down across the frame and taken through the centre hole in the hub. Then back through the next hole to the left around the hub rim, up across the frame and into the hole to the left of the centre in the top rail.

The work was continued in this way until the left hand half of the sun-hub was full. (see figure 39).

38. *Original state of back.*

39. *First stage of first setting.*

42

With some examples it may be necessary to miss out some of the holes on the side rails in order to keep the settings evenly spaced. In such a case the number of holes to be 'lost' is ascertained by comparing the number of holes round the frame with those round the hub.

Next a new length of cane was joined in at the centre of the top rail and the right hand half of the frame was filled in a similar manner.

Now the other cane of each pair of first settings had to be put in and the work was commenced from the first hole to the left of the centre on the top rail. Figures 40 and 41 show the front and the back of the panel with the first setting stage complete. Note how on the back of the frame this method of working gives a single cane between each hole all the way around the work which in turn makes for a neat finish.

As with a normal panel, care must be taken that the canes of each pair of settings are not crossed or twisted but lie parallel to one another throughout their length and are all shiny side up.

Second Settings:

In the sunray pattern the second settings run in semi-circles concentric with the sun-hub itself. They are woven through the first settings in the normal way and are best put in singly leaving adequate 'tails' for later adjustment.

40. *First Settings complete (front view).*

41. *First Settings complete (back view).*

40

41

The work was begun from the first hole to the left of the sun-hub in the bottom rail and a pair of settings were woven round through the first settings to the first hole in the bottom rail to the right of the hub. The work was continued in this way for each of the holes in the bottom rail with each pair of settings describing a larger semi-circle than the last.

When all the holes in the bottom rail had been filled, the work was continued from suitable holes in the side rails until the whole frame had been filled. Figure 42 shows how the pairs of settings should be spaced across the frame. Note also the short settings worked into the top corners.

The method of weaving used is the same as for the standard double setting pattern. The first cane of each pair, (that nearest the hub) going under-over, under-over, etc. The second doing the opposite.

Crossings:

The crossings were woven through the web formed by the settings in the usual manner. However, as the first settings all radiated out from the central sun-hub, one set of crossings curved to the left and one to the right, giving the characteristic 'swirl' effect to the pattern.

Each crossing cane was inserted singly, starting from the sun-hub and working out across the panel to the frame.

The first crossing was woven under the first settings and over the second, curving back towards the left hand side of the frame (figure 43).

42. Second Setting stage complete.

43. First Crossing stage.

46

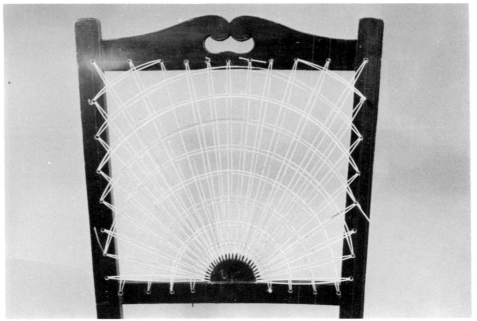

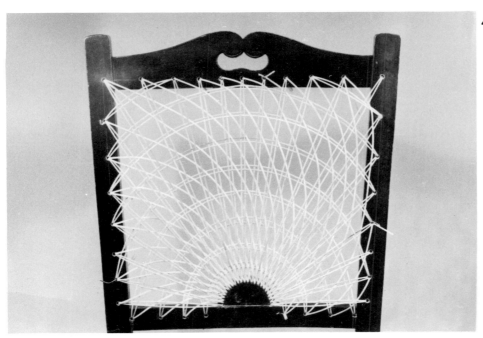

The second crossing was woven over the first settings and under the second, curving towards the right hand side of the frame (figure 44).

On the hub itself care should be taken to ensure that the crossing canes fit neatly together, whilst around the frame, the curve formed by each cane should be continued as far as possible.

On most panels worked in this pattern it is necessary to use additional short lengths of cane to fill in the crossings on the corners.

The panel when completed was pegged and then trimmed, great care being taken when pegging the sun-hub.

The finished chair is shown in figure 45.

44. *Second Crossing stage.*

45. *Completed Chair.*

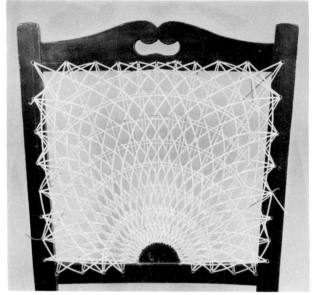

44

45

Spider Back

This beautiful lacquered chair illustrates one of the more unusual techniques used in chair caning. (figures 46 and 47).

The centre medallion is held in place only by the web of cane itself and will always have the same number of holes as the frame surrounding it. This means, of course, that the holes in the medallion are very fine and very close together as with the sun-hub in the previous chapter.

46. *Original condition.*

Preparation:

The old cane and pegs were carefully removed from the frame and medallion which were then cleaned with a damp cloth. No other cleansing agent was used to avoid the possibility of damage to the lacquer.

47. *Close-up of back.*

Next the medallion had to be supported in place before work could begin on the settings. Four lengths of moderately stiff wire were cut and were attached to the medallion through the top, bottom and centre side holes. The other end of each wire was then attached to the corresponding centre hole in each rail of the frame. (see figure 48). With a little adjustment and the use of a tape measure the medallion was fixed securely in the centre of the frame.

48. *Medallion in place.*

Care must be taken that any pattern on the medallion is the right way up!

46

47

48

First Settings:

With the spider-back pattern the first settings radiate out from the centre medallion to the frame of the back. As with the sunray pattern, although double settings are used, one cane of each pair is put in first. In the example shown No. 1 cane was used for the settings, the work being started from the first hole to the left of the supporting wire in the top rail.

A good length of cane was selected and one end inserted into the hole. The other was then brought down across the frame and through the first hole to the left of the top supporting wire in the medallion.

Then it was brought back through the next hole to the left in the medallion and up to the next hole to the left in the top rail.

The work was continued in this way in an anti-clockwise direction, the supporting wires being removed as required, until the frame was filled. (see figure 49).

Continuing with the same cane, the direction of work was now reversed and the second cane of each pair of first settings was added working back clockwise around the frame.

The work was concluded at the centre hole in the top rail and the loose ends were carefully tied in at the back of the frame. The completed first setting stage is shown in figure 50.

The first setting canes should be kept as firm as possible without pulling the medallion out of position.

49. First stage of first setting.

50. First Setting complete.

49

50

Second Settings:

In this example the second settings were woven through the first in the form of a spiral gradually working out from the centre medallion.

Although in the original panel the spiral ran anti-clockwise this is purely a matter of personal preference and as will be seen (figure 52) the new spiral was worked in a clockwise direction.

Work was begun from the lower left hand side of the medallion and a pair of second setting canes was woven round and round through the first settings until the frame was filled.

Figure 51 shows the commencment of the work and figure 52 the second setting stage complete. Note how the last rounds and the corners are worked with short lengths of cane.

The method of weaving used is the same as in the standard double setting pattern. The first cane of each pair, ie. that nearest the medallion, goes under-over, under-over, etc. whilst the second cane of the pair does the opposite.

51.   *Beginning of second setting working.*

52.   *Second setting complete.*

51

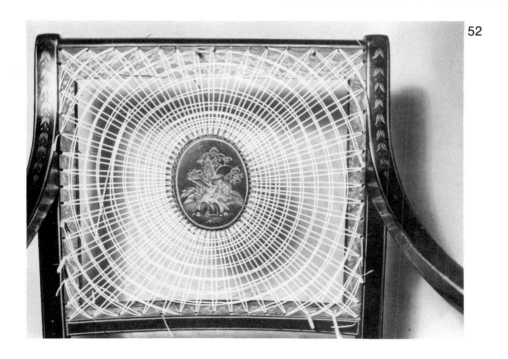

52

Crossings:

As with the sunray pattern, each crossing cane was worked from the centre or hub out to the frame of the back. No. 2 cane was used for this stage.

The first crossing was worked under the first settings and over the second, curving back to the left in an anti clockwise direction. (see figure 53).

The second crossing was worked over the first settings and under the second, curving to the right in a clockwise direction. (figure 54)

Care was taken to space the canes as evenly as possible in the corners of the frame.

When the work was complete all the holes were pegged using centre cane for the frame of the back and very fine slivers of cane for the medallion.

The finished back is shown in figure 55 (see page 59).

53. *First Crossing stage.*

54. *Second Crossing stage.*

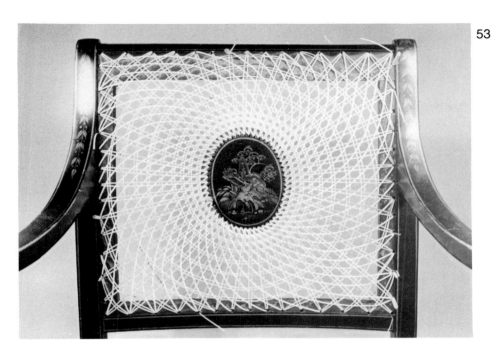

53

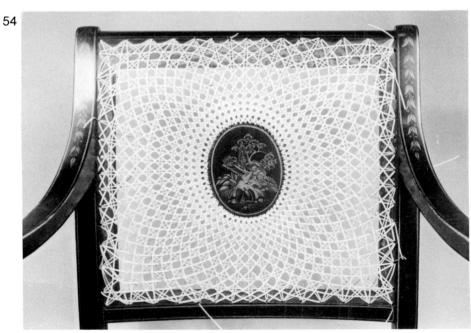

54

Spider Back with Circular Second Settings

In the example shown in figure 56 the second settings, instead of taking the form of a spiral, are woven in concentric circles around the centre medallion.

The method of working used is much the same as for the previous chair but each ring of the second setting is inserted as a seperate length of cane. Where the circle finishes the cane is overlapped for about an inch to an inch and a half, the ends being trimmed off neatly so that they are hidden by the first settings.

These 'joins' in the second settings should, in order to preserve a neat finish, be spaced around the panel of the back.

For example, if the first cane to be inserted is joined above the medallion, the second should be joined below it. The third can then be joined to the right and the fourth to the left.

This pattern can then be repeated through-out the course of the panel.

It is as well to leave the second settings with adequate 'tails' until the work is complete to allow for adjustment to the spacing of the canes if necessary.

55. *Completed Back.*

56. *Spider back with circular second settings.*

55

56

Arm Chair (Bergere)

In chairs of this type (figure 57) the caning holes are drilled in the frame around the edge of each panel as usual, but do not go right the way through the frame to the other side.

This means that although the eventual pattern achieved is the same as in a normal panel, the method of working is different.

The reverse of the panel is shown in figure 58 where it will be noted that there is no evidence of the holes or the usual series of cane loops.

Preparation of Frame:

Once the old cane had been cut from the panel the holes had to be drilled out, care being taken not to damage the chair frame.

A hand or electric drill may be used for this work, a drill bit slightly smaller in diameter than the size of the holes being chosen.

In order to ascertain the depth of hole required use a hand drill on the first hole and work slowly. It is usual to tell by the difference in the feel of the drilling where the old hole stopped, but in any case do not go beyond three quarters of the way through the thinest part of the frame.

For safety's sake a depth stop of some kind should be fitted to the drill before the main work is undertaken. Layer upon layer of sticky tape wound around the drill bit at the required depth will suffice.

Settings:

As the holes do not go right the way through the frame, each pair of settings has to be put in seperately and glued into place. This is best done using an adhesive such as 'Evo-Stick' Woodwork Adhesive. This product is strong

57. Original Panel.

58. Reverse of Panel.

57

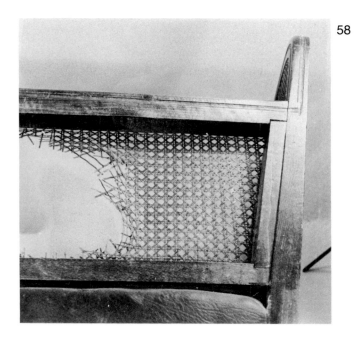

58

and durable, yet excess glue may be wiped away with a damp cloth before it dries.

The first settings should be across the shortest way of the frame and so in this case were worked from top to bottom of the panel.

Two lengths of No. 2 cane were cut slightly longer than required and the last half inch of one end dipped in glue. These ends were then inserted into the first hole in the bottom rail which was then pegged using a metal peg. (Wire nails of appropriate thickness are ideal for this) Care was taken to ensure that the canes were suitably placed in the hole and were the right way up when stretched across the panel.

59.   First Settings.

Wooden or cane pegs obviously cannot be used as they will become irremovably stuck in the holes when the glue dries.

The two canes were now stretched across the frame to the first hole in the top rail and trimmed to allow just enough extra cane to go into the hole. (usually half to three quarters of an inch).

These ends were then glued, inserted and pegged as before, care being taken to keep the canes as tight as possible.

The work was continued in this way across the panel as shown in figure 59 until the frame was filled. The work was then set aside to dry out for 24 hours.

The pegs were then removed and the canes checked to see that they were secure and had not been twisted or reversed.

Now the second settings were inserted in a similar manner, being woven through the first settings and the ends glued into their respective holes and pegged. Again the work was left to dry out.

Crossings and Beading:

The crossings are worked in the normal manner for double setting pattern, the ends being trimmed and inserted into their respective holes. They need not be glued into place except in the corner holes where this should be done.

60. *Method of Beading.*

Four lengths of beading cane (No. 6) were cut to size and a length of couching cane (No. 2) was prepared by cutting into pieces measuring twice the depth of the holes plus one eighth of an inch.

Each piece of couching was now folded in half, shiny side out, and the ends dipped in glue. The beading cane was laid along the course of the holes on its side, with its shiny surface facing away from the panel and each piece of prepared couching was inserted over the beading into its hole and was pegged with centre cane. (figure 60).

Care must be taken to ensure that the couching canes are inserted on the opposite side of the holes from the setting canes, ie. the peg should separate the two. Thus, at the top of the panel they are inserted at the top of the holes, while at the bottom of the panel they go at the bottom of the holes, and so on.

61. *Completed Chair.*

The beading cane may then be folded down flat over the holes it is to cover and glued to the work, the ends being tucked into the corner holes in the usual way.

A series of clamps or a board cut to the size of the panel with a heavy weight on it may be needed to hold the cane in place while the glue dries, but care must to taken not to put any strain on the panel itself.

The completed chair is shown in figure 61.

60

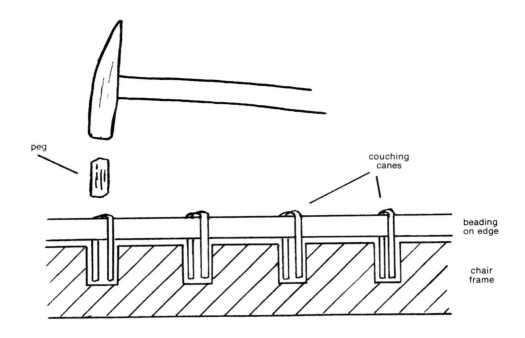

peg

couching
canes

beading
on edge

chair
frame

61

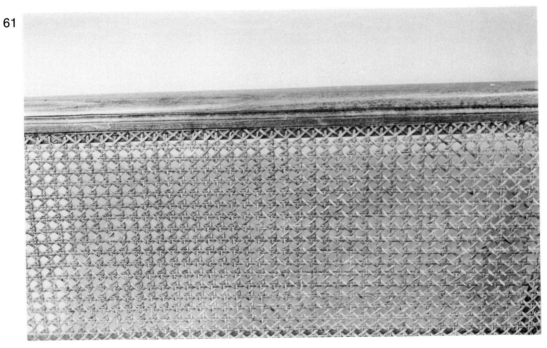

Modern Chair with Cane Webbing Panel

This modern cane dining chair, although in appearance being worked in standard double setting pattern, in fact employs quite a different seating technique.

Upon close examination it will be found that there are no caning holes in the frame but that the seat is cut from a machine-made sheet of 'cane webbing' which is then attached to the frame of the chair.

Cane webbing is supplied by the metre in a number of different widths suitable for a variety of applications. Today it is also popularly used in decorative panels and screens etc. and as an attractive finish applied to wardrobe and cupboard doors.

Figure 63 shows a square piece of webbing as it is cut from the roll.

Around the edge of the seat panel it will be found that there is a fillet of centre cane set into a groove in the frame of the seat and it is this which holds the panel in position.

This fillet is glued into place and therefore must be removed by prising out as much as possible with the blade of an old screwdriver and then cleaning the groove up with a knife and a fine chisel. Care must be taken not to damage the frame of the seat.

A new length of centre cane is prepared large enough in diameter to just fit the groove and long enough to fit snugly around the frame

62. *Chair with cane webbing seat.*

63. *Cane webbing.*

66

62

63

Next a new piece of webbing is cut large enough to just cover the seat frame. This is clamped to the frame along the right hand side and at the front using G-clamps and suitable lengths of wood.

The back and left hand side of the webbing are trimmed to size leaving a margin of about half an inch all round to go down into the groove.

Starting from the centre of the back, work a section of the margin of the webbing down into the groove with the blade of a screwdriver, care being taken not to break or crack any of the canes in the process.

Run glue liberally into the groove, (Evostick Woodworking Adhesive is suitable), and insert the end of the new fillet, working from the centre of the back anti-clockwise, using a mallet to tap the cane into the groove.

To avoid bruising the cane the work is protected with a small piece of thick card, which also keeps the mallet from coming into contact with any excess glue.

Continue in this way as far as possible. Then release the clamps, trim the remainder of the seat, and continue until complete.

Any excess glue should be wiped away with a damp cloth and the seat set aside to dry out.

On a square or shaped seat care must be taken to ensure that the cane fillet does not become cracked or damaged when turning sharp corners etc.

Figure 64 shows a close up of the seat.

64. Close up of seat.

Corner Chair in Rush

This attractive corner chair (figure 65) was in good condition when we received it and the old seat had already been removed. Therefore no preparation work was necessary.

A small bundle of rush was prepared (see chapter 16) choosing a fairly long sample as with a seat of this size (20″ square), the distances to be spanned are quite long.

Method of Work:

A start was made by selecting two rushes of nearly equal length and of a thickness that would produce a rush twist of medium diameter suitable for a seat of this size. (see chapter 16).

The thick end (butt) of one of the selected rushes was attached to the left hand rail of the chair frame about 4″ in from the back.

To do this, the rush was laid across the rail leaving 6–9″ of the butt sticking out beyond the frame. This butt end was then wrapped tightly round the rail, brought up behind the original rush, forward over it and down to be trapped between it and the seat rail. (see figure 66).

65. *Chair frame on arrival.*

66. *Attaching the rush to the seat frame.*

65

66

A second rush was then joined in by wrapping it around the first in the same way as the first was attached to the frame, the butt end being trapped between the two rushes. (see figure 67).

Care was taken to ensure that both 'knots' were as tight as possible to prevent slipping, and that neither rush showed any sign of cracking.

These two rushes form the basis of the 'cord' from which the seat is worked.

The two rushes were then brought forward over the front seat rail so as to lie close up against the inside of the chair leg.

In this position they were then twisted towards the centre of the front rail with the right hand whilst the fingers of the left moulded the rushes together to form a rope.

This was continued until the length of rush lying across the seat frame plus sufficient to pass down the front of the rail and just underneath was smoothly twisted. (figure 68).

Care must be taken to avoid lumps or 'furrows' in the twist and to see that no cracking occurs.

The twisted rush 'cord' was then taken down around the front of the seat rail and back up through the centre of the frame. Then to the left over the front of the left hand rail so as to lie closely behind the left hand front chair leg.

The rush was then again twisted to form a rope, this time towards the centre of the left hand seat rail, until a smooth 'cord' was produced.

67. *Joining in new rush.*

68. *Rush twisted to form a rope.*

67

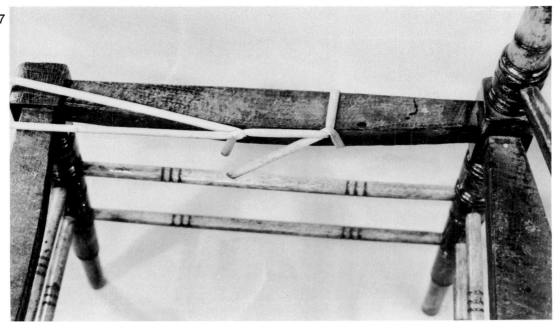

68

It was then taken down around the rail, back up through the frame and over the right hand seat rail. (see figure 69). This forms the first step in the mitre which runs in to the centre of the seat from each corner.

It should be noted that in forming the rope the rush is always twisted towards the centre of the rail over which it is passing and away from the mitre being formed.

It was now necessary to join in a new rush of suitable diameter and this was done as before (see figure 67), so maintaining an even thickness in the subsequent working.

If required a second new rush could be joined in at this stage when the tails of the old rushes would be broken off after the second join.

The rush was now taken over the right hand rail, twisted to form a rope, carried down round the rail, and brought back up through the seat frame.

It was then taken forward over the front rail, again twisted, carried down round the rail and brought up through the seat frame as before.

The same process was repeated around the right hand back leg of the chair and so on round and round the frame, new rushes being added in as required, until two to three inches had been worked over the frame.

The work must be kept tight and each new round of working packed closely against the last. Also care must be taken that where the rush twists form the mitre, they lie smoothly against one another and that one does not ride up over the next.

69. *First Corner complete.*

Any rushes that show a tendency to crack during working must be discarded and as the work proceeds it must be kept square with the frame of the chair.

The underside of the seat should be kept as neat as possible with the butt ends from the joins being tucked in as the seat progresses.

As the seat developed triangular pockets were formed in each corner of the seat frame on either side of the mitre. If left empty, these pockets would cause the seat to loosen with use and sag. Therefore they were carefully packed with waste rush folded to form small flat bundles and pushed well into the corners, care being taken to leave the surface of the seat smooth and even. (figure 70).

The work was now continued as before round and round the frame. From time to time the rush was pegged off as shown in figure 70 and more packing was inserted to keep the seat a good shape.

When the gap left unfilled in the frame was reduced to about two inches, care was taken to ensure that the packing joined across from one pocket to the next adequately so that the final strands would not sink down into the middle of the seat. (see figure 71).

70. *Packing the pockets.*

71. *The packing complete.*

70

71

In these last stages new lengths of rush were joined in in a slightly different manner so as to avoid too many knots in the rapidly diminishing gap.

With this method the butt of the new rush is twisted around the old rushes two or three times where they come under the existing work (see figure 72) The twist must run in the same direction as the twist on the next seat rail to be worked over or else it will come undone. This method can only be used when a part of the rush twist is being replaced.

When inserting the last few strands of the seat it was necessary to use the hook to ease the rushes up through the centre of the work (see figure 73). The hook is pushed carefully down through the gap left in the seat centre, and hooked around the bundle of rushes leaving enough slack to draw them gently through.

Care must be taken not to damage the adjacent work and once a loop of rush is pulled through the hook is discarded and the remaining length of the rush drawn up with the fingers.

Each rail was filled as tightly as possible to avoid gaps forming when the work dried out. The seat being square, it was found that the four mitres met neatly in the middle of the seat when complete.

72. *Joining in new rush 2nd method.*

73. *Using the hook.*

72

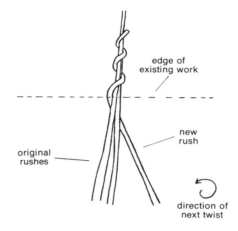

edge of
existing work

new
rush

original
rushes

direction of
next twist

73

To finish off the work the last loop of rush was taken over the chair frame in the usual way and the ends were tucked neatly away between the rushes making up the underside of the seat using the blunt end of the hook. (see figure 74).

The seat being now complete, the chair was turned over and the underside of the seat checked for any remaining ends protruding through the rush. These were tucked away using the blunt end of the hook to push them out of sight.

The finished chair was stood aside in a cool place away from direct sunlight, to dry out.

No attempt should be made to hasten this process or undue shrinkage of the rush may occur, resulting in the seat becoming loose and wearing badly.

During the drying process, in some cases where the atmosphere tends to be damp, a slight mould may form on the rush surfaces. This may be brushed gently off using a clothes brush, working with the line of the strands in the seat. Never brush across the strands, but always from the centre out towards each rail in turn. The underside may be dealt with in a similar manner.

Once the seat is thoroughly dry, after up to about a fortnight, no further trouble will be experienced.

The completed chair is shown in figure 75.

74. *Finishing off.*

75. *Completed chair.*

80

74

75

Rush Ladderback

This lovely old ladderback chair was one of a set of six brought in to us for reseating. The old seats were still in place and these had to be cut out with a sharp knife before work could begin. (See chapter 18)

Once the seat had been removed the frame was checked for loose joints and damage to the rails (see chapter 19).

Figure 76 shows the frame cleared and ready for working.

Method of Working:

With this chair the seat was not square but was considerably wider at the front than at the back. Thus, in order that the mitres should still form smooth straight lines, this difference in width had to be gradually evened up during the early stages of working.

This was done by weaving extra twists of rush around the front of the frame in the following manner.

The rush was joined to the left hand rail of the frame as in the previous chapter and the same pattern of working was followed until approximately one inch of the weaving was complete.

The rush was then pegged off against the right hand rail (after having worked around the right hand front leg), and new rushes were tied into the work on the left hand side of the frame (see figure 77).

These new rushes were then worked around the front of the frame in the usual manner, passing over the front rail, up through the frame, over the left rail, up through the frame and so on.

76. *Frame ready for working.*

77. *Working extra rushes around the front of the frame.*

76

77

When the new strands caught up with the pegged off 'tails' of the original working, both groups of rushes were gathered together and continued over the back rail as one. Any short rush tails were discarded and new lengths joined in as required.

The work then proceeded around the back of the frame in the normal way and again round the front until the rush could be pegged off against the right hand rail as before.

The process was then repeated, adding new rushes on the left of the frame, working around the front of the chair, picking up the tails of the old rush and continuing over the back rail.

The number of times that this has to be done to even up the work depends upon the shape of the chair frame.

With each extra round added, the distance remaining unworked on the back and front rails should be measured and compared. This should be done with the rush pegged off against the left hand rail over the original starting point of the work.

When the distance still to be worked on each rail (back and front) was found to be the same, the extra rounds of working at the front were discontinued. Figure 78 shows the chair at this stage, with the rush pegged off in the correct position for measurement to take place.

78. *Chair with working at front and back evened up.*

The seat was now continued in the usual manner, working round and round the frame, packing out the pockets formed in the corners as the work progressed.

With a seat of this shape the side rails are completed well before the front and back rails and the remaining gap must be filled working in a figure of eight pattern from front to back of the chair.

In this way a straight 'bar' is formed in the middle of the seat joining the four mitres together. The handle of the hook was used to push the crossing point of these final loops of working closely together so that the work remained square.

When working this last section, care was taken to always twist the rushes in the same direction, i.e. if working from left to right, always twist towards the right hand rail, in the direction in which the work is proceeding, and vice versa.

If this is not done a 'step' will develop in the bar which will spoil the appearance of the work.

The finished chair is shown in figure 79.

79.   *Completed chair.*

86

Drop-in Seat

This chair was one of a set of six brought in to us for restoration and reseating.

The seat itself was worked over a light wooden frame with raised corners to hold the rush, which was then dropped into the frame of the chair. (Figure 80).

With this type of seat there is often very little clearance between the seat frame and the frame of the chair and thus a very fine diameter rush twist must be used.

This in turn means that only fine rushes are of use for this type of work as each twist must be made up of at least two strands.

If there is insufficient clearance for the thickness of rush available it is sometimes possible to plane down the seat frame between the corners with a surform plane and a file. If this is done the edges of the frame must be left rounded to avoid damage to the rush later when the chair is in use.

80. Chair with drop-in seat.

The seat was worked in the same manner as the ladderback in the previous chapter and was replaced frequently in the chair frame to make sure that it still fitted.

Figure 81 shows the frame ready for working and figures 82 and 83 the work evened up and completed respectively.

If, despite all precautions, difficulty is experienced in refitting the seat, a little extra clearance may be obtained by very gently tapping along the edge of the rush work, where it turns over the seat frame, with a light hammer. (Be sure that the hammer head is clean.)

This must be done only when the seat is still damp or cracking will occur.

When complete, the seat was left to dry out in the frame.

81. Seat frame.

82. The work evened up.

83. Completed seat.

81

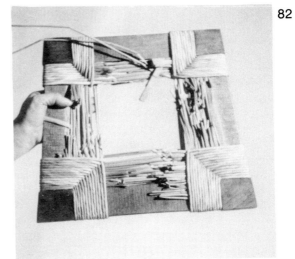

82

83

Working in Cane

Types of Cane used for Seating:

Two basic types of cane are used in chair seating. Flat seating cane, which comes in a variety of widths and is used for weaving the web of cane itself.

Centre cane, which is circular in section, is supplied in a range of different diameters, and is used for pegging the seat.

Different widths of seating cane are distinguished by a code of numbers, No. 1 being the finest normally available, Nos. 2 and 3 are the most commonly used sizes, for settings and crossings respectively. No. 4 is suitable where a slightly heavier cane is required, in single setting pattern for example. No. 6 is used for beading. One side of the seating cane is shiny, the other dull, the shiny side forms the surface of the seat.

With the centre cane Sizes 8 and 12 are the most commonly used, the latter being the larger.

Cane is generally supplied in hanks weighing ¼ kilo although some suppliers do offer smaller quantities. The best quality available should always be chosen.

Patterns used in Chair Caning:

The most common and probably the most satisfactory pattern used for seats is the 'Double Setting' pattern. This is both strong and durable and consists of interwoven pairs of canes running from front to back and from side to side of the seat, together with single canes woven diagonally (see figure 84).

'Single Setting' pattern is also sometimes used but has not the same strength and rigidity (figure 85).

84.   Double Setting pattern.

85.   Single Setting pattern.

92

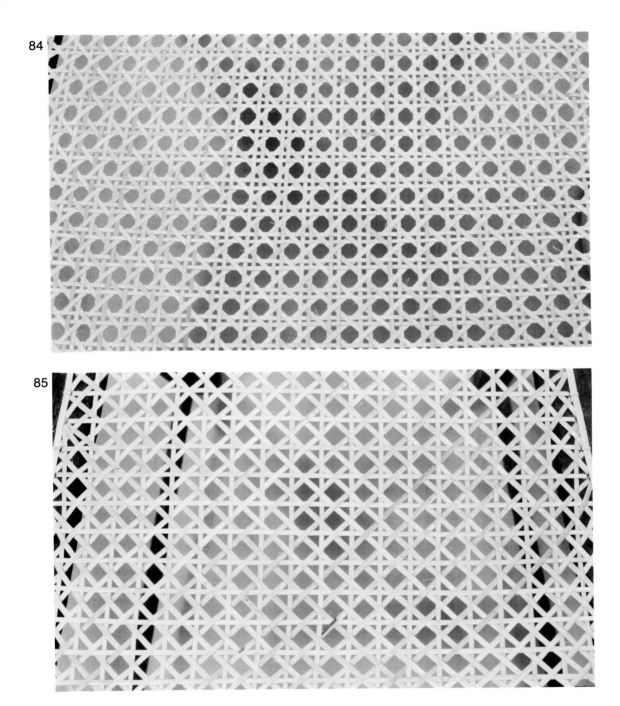

A number of more elaborate and fancy patterns are used in chair backs and decorative panels and for applications where strength is not of primary importance.

Figure 86 opposite, shows a selection of hanks of cane together with a rather attractive 'grasshopper' chair that is worked in the same way as a normal curved panel. i.e. the first settings would run from side to side of the chair.

Preparation of Cane:

When the cane is drawn from the hank it should be carefully examined for faults and flaws. These may take the form of thin or weak places in the cane, of patches of discolouration, or of weak or brittle 'joints' in the material. Likewise, split and damaged sections should be avoided.

The cane may be worked either in the dry state or after being wrapped in a damp cloth for half an hour or so. Long strands should be used for settings etc., whilst short lengths may be set aside for couching.

86. *A Selection of cane.*

Points to Watch:

Always be sure that the cane is kept the right way up throughout the working of the seat.

Check regularly that canes are not crossed or twisted when working settings.

The cane should not be twisted in the holes or underneath the seat.

Check knots for tightness and see they do not get pulled up into the holes.

Keep the finish as neat as possible both on top and underneath the seat.

When pegging, use pegs of correct thickness. i.e. they must be tight enough that they cannot be pressed in with the fingers, but not so tight that they split when tapped in with the hammer.

87. Applying stain to the seat of music stool.

Staining:

When complete the work may be stained down either to match a given colour or merely to take away the 'new' look of the cane. A spirit stain, such as Colron may be used and is applied with a soft brush. One or more coats may be needed depending upon the depth of colour required.

The surface of the panel may then be rubbed over with a polish cloth to improve the finish.

Figures 87 and 88 show stain being applied to a cane seated music stool. This was worked in the same way as the bentwood chairs but the seat had to be removed from the frame of the stool to gain access to some of the holes.

88. Applying stain to underside of the seat.

87

88

Chairs with Fillets:

It will be found that in some chairs, instead of the cane loops being visible on the back of the frame, they are set in a groove and are concealed with a fillet of wood.

At first sight it can sometimes be very difficult to see such a fillet as the cracks around the edges become filled with polish. Therefore examine the back of each rail very closely before assuming that the panel is worked in 'Bergere' style.

Before work on the panel can begin the fillet must be gently prised out of the groove. It is often not possible to do this without irreparable damage to the fillet itself, but great care should be taken not to damage the edges of the groove in the frame.

When the work is complete, the fillet may be replaced or if badly damaged renewed.

When working panels of this nature keep the canes as flat in the groove as possible and take care that the knots are neat and do not stand out too far from the frame.

Figure 89 shows a rocking chair with cane panels in seat and back. The seat panel was worked in the normal manner but the back panel had a fillet of wood let into the frame and this had to be removed (figure 90).

In this case the fillet was very obvious as the chair had been stripped before arriving at the workshop.

89. *Rocking Chair.*

90. *Removing the fillet.*

98

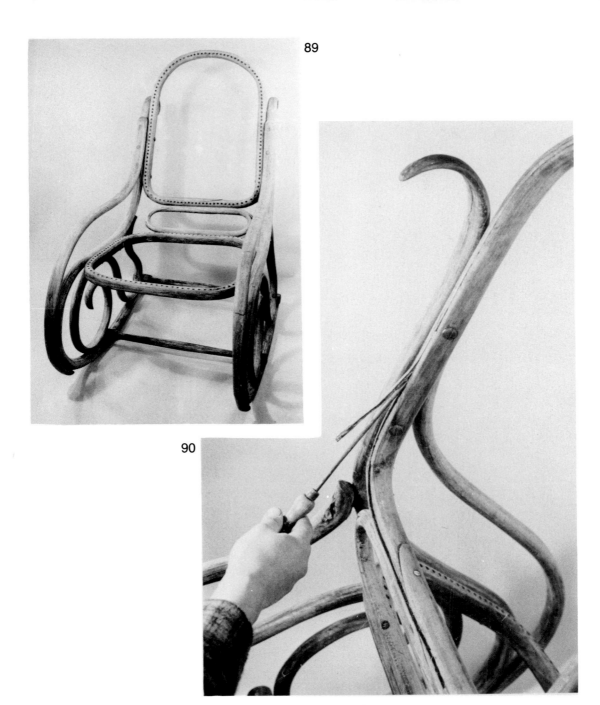

89

90

Working in Rush

Preparation:

Before starting work the rush must be prepared by damping it down and leaving it aside to mellow. This may be done in one of two ways depending upon the quality of the rush and prevailing atmospheric conditions.

With a good quality sample, unless the weather is very hot and dry, it is sufficient to sprinkle the bundle of rush with water (preferably rainwater) from a watering can and then wrap it in a damp cloth until soft and pliable.

The length of time needed for the rush to mellow can vary considerably but will usually be from one to three hours. When a single rush can be twisted and bent in any direction without cracking it is ready for use.

For rush that is harder and more brittle it is better to soak it for from one to four hours in a trough (this can be easily made with polythene sheeting and a few pieces of wood) until it is pliable, and then to lay it aside in a cool place to drain for about half an hour.

Seating rush is generally supplied in large bundles or 'bolts' but only sufficient for the day's work should be soaked down at a time. If damp rush has to be left over night it should be spread out in a dry place and then re-damped the next morning until it is again workable.

Rush can only be damped down two or at the most three times as it will then become discoloured and 'sticky' and must be discarded.

Figure 91 shows a typical bolt of rush. Note the seed heads and sheaths still attached to the rushes in the foreground. The two spindle-back chairs are worked in the same way as the ladderback.

91. *Bolt of rush.*

100

Before the rush is put into the seat the seed head should be removed from the tip and the sheath must be stripped from the butt. Any pieces that are damaged or cracked should be set aside and used later for packing out the seat pockets.

Points to Watch:

When twisting the rush to form a cord or rope, remember that you are aiming to mould the strands into one, rather than merely twisting them together. Use the fingers of the left hand to mould the cord into shape while applying the twist with the right hand (see figure 92).

Keep the work as tight as possible taking care, particularly under the seat, that successive rounds of working do not ride up one over the other.

Discard any rushes that crack while being worked as these will weaken the finished seat. Remember that the whole seat on a square frame is one continuous thread so that a weak place at only one point can be enough to ruin the work.

Ensure that each round of working is pushed tightly up against the last on each rail as the seat progresses.

Make sure that the work remains square throughout the whole process of weaving, that the rush twists fit snugly together where they cross on the mitres, and do not ride one over the other.

92. Forming the twist.

While the seat is drying out watch for any sign of a mould forming between the rush twists and if necessary remove gently with a clothes brush, working from the centre of the seat out along the strands to each rail (figure 93).

93. *Brushing off the seat.*

Selecting for Size:

Before a seat is commenced consideration should be given to the thickness of rush to be used.

For a small chair, or one with a drop-in seat a fine twist is required and therefore a fine rush should be selected.

On the other hand, for a larger seat, a thicker twist is not only more durable but also looks more in keeping with the proportion of the seat.

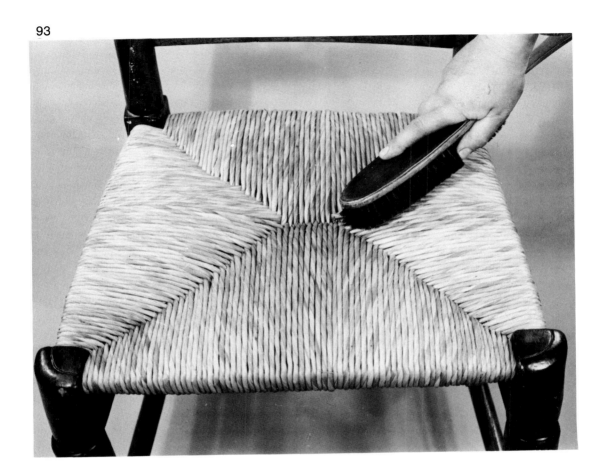

Tools

For Cane Work:

A light hammer for use in clearing the frame and for pegging.

A clearing tool to act as a 'prodder' for removing the old cane and pegs from the holes. A range of tools of different sizes can be simply made from such items as wire nails with the points filed down, straight skewers cut down as required, etc.

A sharp knife, such as a Stanley Knife, for cutting out the old seat. Also for shaping pieces of centre cane when making pegs etc.

A pair of good quality scissors for trimming off unwanted ends of cane.

A pair of Pincers or Clippers for cutting up pieces of centre cane for pegging the seat.

Also useful at times are the tools found on a typical penknife such as a spike and pointed nail file.

94. Tools for canework.

For Rush Work:

Again a sharp knife is essential for cutting out the old seat. Even very old, frayed, rush is surprisingly hard to cut through.

A rather heavier hammer and an old screwdriver will be found useful in removing rush from behind the bars that are sometimes found around old seats (see chapter 18).

Two spring-type wooden clothes pegs will be needed for pegging off the rush while working the seat.

A large crochet hook (size 7 is ideal) for drawing the rush through the seat in the later stages of working.

A pair of scissors may also be used occasionally though it is usual to snap off ends of waste rush rather than to cut them.

95. Tools for rushwork.

94

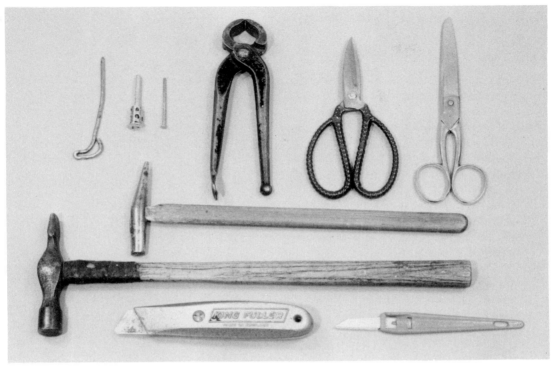

95

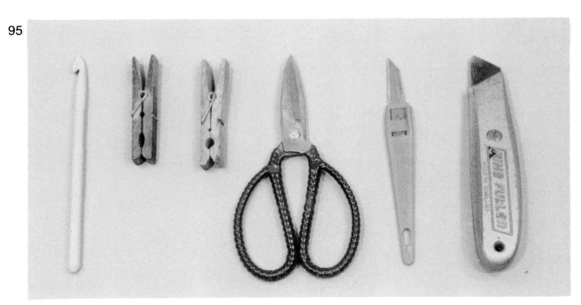

Frame Preparation

Cane Panels:

Before removing the old canework from the frame it is a good idea to make a note of the sizes of cane used, the type and size of the beading, and any unusual factors in the method of weaving.

If the new panel has to be matched for colour then the old web of cane should be kept for reference purposes.

Cut around the panel close to the inside of the frame with a sharp knife, taking care not to damage the wood.

Using a clearing tool of suitable thickness for the size of holes, (it should be about three quarters the diameter of the hole) and a light hammer, clear the old cane and pegs from the holes around the frame (see figure 96).

Work from underneath the frame of the panel, remembering that in the corners, particularly with some types of chair seat, the holes may run through the frame at an angle.

Also, in some chairs, the corner holes of the seat are 'blind' and do not come right the way through the frame. Sometimes the old cane can be pulled out from the top with a pair of pliers, otherwise it must be carefully removed with a hand drill (figure 97).

Once all the holes are clear the frame should be cleaned using a little turpentine, or, if the wood has become bleached or discoloured, a little spirit stain of suitable colour.

Finally the structure of the frame should be checked for loose joints and rails, for damaged caning holes or other defects. There is no point in renewing the canework if the frame itself is in poor shape.

96. *Clearing the caning holes.*

97. *Using the drill.*

108

96

97

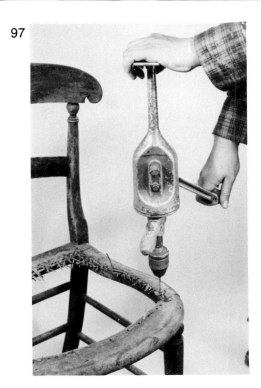

Rush Seats:

For cutting out the old seat a very sharp pointed knife, such as a Stanley knife, is essential.

Start from the back of the right hand rail and cut closely around the inside of the frame using a sawing action (see figure 98).

When complete this process releases the entire seat from the frame, when it can be pushed down through the centre of the chair and discarded.

In some chairs, as with the example shown, narrow wooden bars are fitted around the edges of the seat. No attempt should be made to remove these before cutting out the old rush as they easily split.

In such cases, once the top of the seat has been cut round, the chair should be turned over and the rush levered out from behind the bars as shown in figure 99. An old screwdriver is ideal for this task.

Once all the rush has been loosened the seat may be removed as before by pushing it down through the centre of the chair frame.

The bars may now be tapped gently in towards the frame when the nail heads holding them in place will be revealed. The nails may now be pulled out with the pincers. In stubborn cases a hacksaw blade can be slipped down between the bar and the frame and the nails cut through. The cut nail ends must then be filed down smooth.

There is usually a large accumulation of dirt and grit around the seat frame and this should be scraped away with a knife, paying particular attention to the corners where the legs and rails meet.

The frame should be checked for loose joints or cracked rails and any rough places on the rails should be filed down.

98. *Cutting out the seat.*

99. *Levering out the rush from behind the bars.*

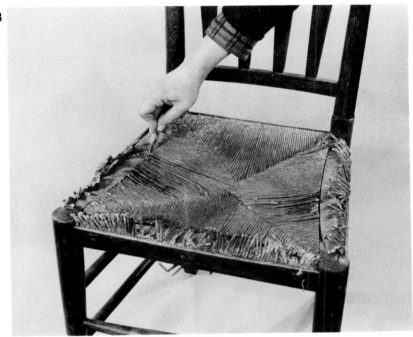

98

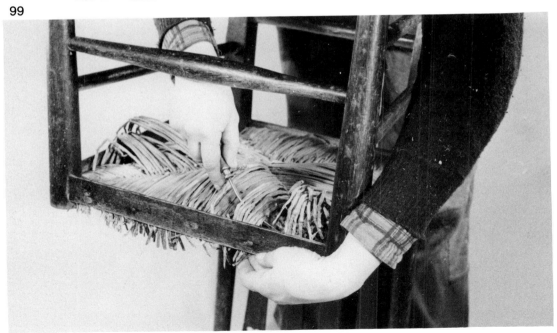

99

Repairs and Restoration

Most chairs needing reseating require only minor repairs or restoration before the new seat is begun.

Loose Joints:

The most common structural fault that is likely to be met with is where the glue holding the frame together has perished allowing the joints to become loose.

In such a case the loose joints should be gently knocked apart using a mallet, protecting the surface of the wood with a piece of thick card or some rag.

Take care to mark top, bottom, right, left etc. on rails where this is not obvious and lay the various parts of the frame out carefully in order.

Any old glue still adhering to the ends of the rails etc. can be removed with a file until all the joints fit together smoothly and easily.

Figures 100 and 101 show a small rush seated side chair where the frame joints were loose and had to be reglued.

100. Rush chair with loose frame.

101. Chair repaired and reseated.

100

101

The spindle back chairs shown in figure 102 also needed the leg joints and some of the rails reglued.

While the glue dried the frame was held tight using simply contrived cramps as shown in figure 103.

Care should be taken when working with very old chairs as the wood tends to become dried out with age and therefore more brittle.

Careless use of the mallet or undue tightening of the cramps in such cases can be disastrous.

Where one or two joints only are loose and the frame cannot easily be knocked apart it is often possible to run enough glue into the joint to effect a repair.

102. Spindle-back chair showing loose leg joints.

103. Frame glued and cramped.

102

103

General Repairs:

With rush seats it will sometimes be found on removing the old rush that one of the seat rails is cracked.

It is a relatively simple task to fashion a new rail out of hardwood using chisels and a surform plane. Copy the original shape as exactly as possible.

With cane seats it will sometimes happen that a split develops along the line of the caning holes. Glue can be run into the split and the rail supported by screws driven through from inside the frame between the holes.

Figure 104 shows a close up of the leg of the spindle back chair shown in figures 102 and 103. A portion of wood was broken out of the top of the leg joint and this had to be replaced. The damaged surfaces were filed flat and a new piece of wood with the grain running in the right direction was shaped to fit and glued into place. When dry the excess wood was trimmed back with a fret saw (figure 105) and the work sandpapered, stained and polished.

104. Damaged leg joint.

105. Trimming off excess wood.

104

105

Glossary of Terms

Cane:

Settings;   The canes running from front to back and from side to side of the panel in the basic pattern of weaving.

Crossings;   The canes running diagonally across the panel and woven through the settings.

Beading;   The cane running around the edge of some panels concealing the caning holes.

Couching;   The cane used to hold the beading in place.

Web;   The interwoven lattice of canes making up the seat or panel.

Rush:

Bolt;   Large bundle of rush as purchased from suppliers.

Butt;   The thick end of the individual rush.

Tip;   The thin end.

Some Suppliers' Addresses

There are many small shops supplying craft materials of various kinds but particularly with the rush, it may be difficult to find exactly what you require locally.

The following firms will supply by post and will send price lists upon request.

Daron Crafts
Rosewood Cottage
Horsham Road
Mid Holmwood
Dorking
Surrey

Dryad Ltd.
P.O. Box 38
Northgates
Leicester
LE1 9BU

Fred Aldous Ltd.
P.O. Box 135
37 Lever Street
Manchester M60 1UX

Another book in the same series:

Restoring Antique Furniture — a practical guide

by Richard Gethin

A practical manual for the person who wants to restore old furniture, but who has no specialised woodworking skills and only standard woodworking tools. Richard Gethin, who started out as an amateur restorer but who now works professionally for antique dealers, takes the reader through many restoring jobs. Included are chapters on replacing veneer, reglueing chairs, replacing drawer runners, replacing wood that is missing on a table top and much more.

Restoring Antique Furniture — a practical guide is very fully illustrated so that the amateur restorer can easily follow the work.